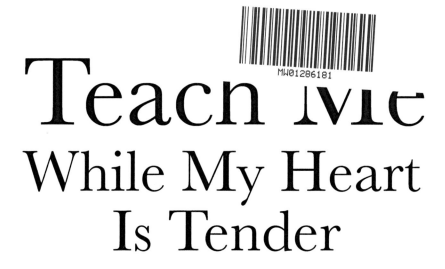

Teach Me
While My Heart
Is Tender

Read Aloud Stories of
Repentance and Forgiveness

Andrea Schwartz

Chalcedon/Ross House Books
Vallecito, CA

This book is dedicated to
Judy Rogers
who has a heart for children
and their salvation

Teach me while my heart is tender;
Tell me all that I should know
And even through the years I will remember
No matter where I go!

(from her song "Why Can't I See God?")

Contents

The People in the Mirror

Preston walked out of his bedroom on the way to eat his favorite breakfast – oatmeal. There was that boy again. He showed up every time Preston passed by the mirror. Today his curiosity got the better of him. "Mom, who is that kid?"

"Which kid, Pres?" his mom replied only half-paying attention.

"The one in the hallway."

His mother looked at her three and a half-year-old son and started to laugh. But she saw that he wasn't joking. "Show me," she said.

Preston jumped down off the kitchen stool, took his mom by the hand, and led her to the hallway inside their two-bedroom apartment. "That kid," he said, "the one with the mom who looks like you."

His mother was in a playful mood. "Oh, those are the people who live in the mirror. I was wondering when you would notice them."

"Do you know the boy's name?" asked Preston.

"No, but he is probably your age." She tried very hard not to laugh.

"How come we only see him sometimes? I mean he is never anywhere else except the bathroom. Do you think he sees me?" Preston scratched his head, trying to act like the detectives on T.V.

"The people in the mirror have their own lives to lead. We see them, and they see us only a small part of the day. When you are eating your breakfast, that boy is eating his. You just can't see him – and he can't see you, except when you're at the mirror."

"Oh, I see. We just see each other sometimes. Did you know that his dad looks like Daddy?"

"Isn't that amazing?" his mother chuckled. "Now go and finish breakfast."

Preston didn't think much more about this until a couple of days later when he was sharing his new found information with his father. His mother had briefed his father about the "people" in the mirror.

Dad played along as Preston embellished his tale with all sorts of things the family in the mirror did. In fact, he even let his dad know that the father in the mirror was going to take the little boy to the park Saturday and out for hamburgers at Nations.

His father said that the dad in the mirror was very generous and acted as though he did not understand the "hint" Preston was giving him.

A month later, the boy in the mirror showed up while Preston and his mom were in a store shopping. Preston was surprised because, until now, he had only seen him at home. Preston wanted to see if he could get the other boy finally to talk to him.

Preston put his face on the mirror and began to whisper, "My name is Preston Bentley."

He was shocked! The boy in the mirror was trying to talk with him at the same time. But Preston couldn't hear him.

When his mother saw him touching the mirror with his mouth, she told him to stop it and get away from the mirror.

"But, Mom, I wasn't talking to a stranger. We know that kid," Preston offered in his own defense. His mother was annoyed and told him to stop touching the mirror with his mouth.

4

When he got home, he took out his toy trucks and sat in front of the mirror. He wasn't really playing. He was spying on that kid to see what he would do. Suddenly, he stopped staring into the mirror and ran to the living room. "There are no people in the mirror," he announced, "That kid is me."

His dad kept a straight face and asked, "Are you sure?"

Preston giggled, "That kid is me."

His mother smiled and congratulated Preston for being such a smart boy. "I knew you'd figure it out eventually," she said.

His father explained, "When your mom told me about the people in the mirror, I thought she was being mean to tease you like that. But she explained that she wanted to give you a chance to figure it out for yourself. She thought it would be helpful to you to learn to figure things out."

Preston nodded. "So what do we call that boy?"

"Your reflection. What you see when you go up by a mirror or a window or TV set is your reflection. It looks like you – only backwards," explained his mom as she walked Preston in front of the mirror.

Years went by and Preston and his parents moved into a house. Every now and then, someone would make a reference to the people in the mirror and they would all laugh. One day, Preston was told that he was going to be a big brother. He was excited watching his mom get bigger and bigger as the months passed.

When he held his infant sister for the first time, he smiled and said, "I'm going to tell her about the people in the mirror. Jessie, there are these people in the mirror who look like us and do the same things we do, but we just only see them at special times." Preston felt very grown up playing this joke on his day-old sister.

"You're going to have to wait until she's old enough to talk. She can't understand you now," his mom explained.

Preston often told Jessie about the people in the mirror. His parents were amused at how eager he was to trick her. When she was about three, he told his mom to watch while he tricked Jessie about the people in the mirror.

"Hey, Jessie, come here. I want to introduce you to someone. See that little girl wearing pink pants like yours? She belongs to the family in the mirror."

Jessie looked at Preston, looked at the mirror, and walked away. She said, "Preston, there are no people in the mirror. That's just my complexion."

Preston was dumbfounded. Who had told his sister this? He felt betrayed. "And, it's not your complexion, Silly; it's your reflection."

Jessie ran to play in her room. Preston asked his mom, "Did you tell her about that?"

"No, Honey, I didn't. I guess she figured it out all by herself."

Jessie poked her head out of her room and stuck her tongue out at her brother. Preston was angry now.

Mrs. Bentley realized she had some "mending" to do.

"Pres, I need to ask for your forgiveness. When you were little, I wanted you to learn things for yourself. I led you to believe there were people in the mirror because I realized you would eventually figure out that the people you saw were reflections, not real people. I wanted you to learn that even though someone tells you something, you often have to investigate yourself to see if it is true. No matter what my reasons were, I still told you something that was not true. I misled you years ago and gave you a bad example. I was wrong to do that and I ask your forgiveness. Your sister has learned some things much faster than you have because she has had the benefit of having a wonderful older brother. You have been a good teacher."

Preston was still mad. When his mom went to hug him, he pulled away. She thought it best to give him some time. She realized that she needed her husband's help in the matter. She called him at work and they agreed that he would call Preston.

When the phone rang, Preston's mom asked him to answer it. Preston was surprised because usually she did not allow him to answer the phone. It was his father.

"Hey, Pres, how's it going?" his father asked.

Preston was so excited about answering the phone that he forgot he was upset.

His father continued, "Son, your mom told me you are upset with her. When she first told you the story about the people in the mirror, I thought it was a bad idea but I went along with her. You were so good-natured when you found out the truth, I didn't think much more about it. I need to ask for your forgiveness, too.

"We both misled you back then. Your mother told me she asked for your forgiveness, but you wouldn't give it."

Preston was silent. His dad continued, "The Bible says, 'Be kind to one another, tenderhearted, forgiving one another, just as God in Christ forgave you.' That is from the book of Ephesians."

Preston felt so grown up having this kind of conversation on the phone with his dad. "I forgive you and Mom, but I don't forgive Jessie."

"What do you have to forgive Jessie for?" asked his dad.

"For thinking she's so smart and making me feel bad."

"Jessie didn't do anything wrong. Just because she did not fall for the joke is no reason to be mad at her."

"But if finding out there weren't any people in the mirror didn't bother me back when I was little, why does it bother me now?"

"That's what is wrong with teasing someone. It may seem funny when you do it, but often people get hurt. And, it can backfire on the person who jokes in this way and make him or her appear mean. That's why your mother feels badly right now, because she knows she hurt you."

Preston did not want his mom to be sad. He realized that he did not feel angry anymore. "Thanks, for talking with me, Dad. I think I should go and talk with Mom. See you later."

Preston went into the laundry room, took his mom by the hand, and brought her to the mirror. "The boy in the mirror wants the mom in the mirror to know that he forgives her." Preston chuckled. His mom bent down and gave her son the hug she had been waiting to give him.

"Mom, I talked with Dad and he explained that sometimes teasing can backfire.

"Just the same, I hope that you will continue to do things that make me laugh. I actually like it. I hope you don't stop. And I hope I can continue to answer the phone when it rings. Can I?"

She looked at her son with pretended shock. "What did you say?"

"Oops, I forgot. May I continue to answer the phone when it rings?"

"Sure. But if the mother in the mirror calls, tell her I'm busy doing the laundry."

More Than Sorry

Darius Pomeroy sat on his bed waiting for his father to come home. His mother had been very angry with him and had sent him to his room. He had never seen her like this before. He didn't see what the big deal was. It's not as if his sister was permanently hurt or anything!

Earlier in the day, Darius's mom had asked him to watch the baby while she showered. Darius liked his babysitting jobs. His mom was very generous when it came to paying him. A quarter here, a dollar there, and before too long he would have enough money for the next set of action figures he wanted so badly.

Darius's parents were not like some of his friends' moms and dads. They did not buy things for him whenever he wanted them. He either had to use some of his birthday or Christmas money or save from what he earned for helping out around the house. That was different from some of his other buddies. They had tons more stuff than they could possibly ever use and they often were bored with all their toys or video games.

Darius's infant sister began to cry before his mom was out of the shower. He tried all the things he could, but she would not stop. This was getting annoying. Since he was supposed to keep her quiet, he tried jumping around to distract her and make her laugh. It wasn't working. So, he thought he should just speak very sternly at her. "Be quiet, Jocelyn. Nobody wants to hear you cry." Still nothing.

Darius remembered that the boys at the pool used to roll up their towels and snap them at each other. He had always wanted to try that, but never had anyone to practice on. Today seemed like the perfect time. Besides, Jocelyn was only three months old. She wouldn't be able to tell on him.

It took a couple of tries before he got the knack of how to get a good snap. Now he was glad that J-lyn was still crying. He had the perfect plan to get her to stop.

After the first snap, she seemed so surprised that she didn't make any noise at all. *Hey, this really works!* thought Darius, so he did it again. This time the baby made a small whimpering noise and Darius was afraid she might start crying again. So, just to make sure, he gave it another snap and this time he landed the best hit of all. However, Jocelyn changed her tune ... and loudly!

Darius's mom knew that she was taking too long in her shower. She could hear that the baby was crying, but she was grateful that her son (six and a half years older than his sister) was a good boy who gladly took care of Jocelyn. When she heard the cries get louder, she hurried and got dressed. She thought, *I should get out there and relieve him of duty. What a great kid I've got!*

Just as she was turning the corner, she saw Darius whip his sister in the face with the rolled up towel. She was horrified. She could barely talk.

Darius did not see his mother come in the room. The baby's cries were so loud he couldn't even hear himself giggle with delight with all the fun he was having. He turned around and saw the look of rage on his mom's face.

In a very slow and deliberate tone, she said, "Darius, get to your room!" At the same time, she grabbed the baby, and began to comfort her.

Darius heard his mom sing to Jocelyn as she walked her around her room and then put her back in her crib. He heard his mom's muffled voice and he knew she was on the phone with his dad. He could not imagine what was in store for him when his dad got home from work at 9 o'clock. He knew things were not going to be very pleasant because his mom did not call him for dinner. Only visits to the bathroom were allowed.

Darius told himself that he was just trying to do what his mom had asked and that she had misunderstood the whole thing. However, he found it hard to believe his excuse, let alone be able to convince his dad. He kept practicing his defense over and over. *I didn't mean to hurt her. I thought she would like it. Besides, I only did it one time!*

Finally, Darius fell asleep. He woke up when his dad walked into his room and turned on the light. He pretended to be asleep, hoping that his dad would wait until morning to have this dreaded conversation. No such luck. "Darius, sit up I want to talk with you," his father said.

Darius slowly sat up in bed, rubbing his eyes, hoping his dad would think he was too sleepy to talk. However, his dad picked up the chair on the other side of the room and brought it near the bed. He knew his dad was taking this seriously because he hadn't taken time to change his clothes – he had come right in to see him.

"Son, we need to talk about today."

"I know," said Darius holding back tears. Then he burst out, "I'm sorry, Daddy. I'm really sorry." With that, he jumped out of bed and hugged his dad.

His father placed Darius back on the bed. "You know, Son, it isn't enough to be sorry."

"But shouldn't I be sorry?" he asked between sobs.

"You need to be more than sorry. Being sorry means that you feel bad about what happened. And, why shouldn't you? Your mom is angry with you, your sister was traumatized, you are hungry because you had no dinner, and you are probably trying to figure out what your punishment will be. I'm not surprised you are sorry. There is a word for that. It is called remorse."

Darius seemed relieved that his dad was speaking so calmly. It sounded as though there was more his dad wanted to say. Before his dad could continue, Darius said, "Daddy, I will be a good boy from now on. I promise."

"The Bible tells us, Darius, that none of us are good. In fact, you just made a promise that you can't keep."

Darius looked puzzled. He wanted to promise again, but held his tongue.

"Do you remember the definition of sin from your catechism?"

Darius shook his head and slowly recited, "Sin – is – any – want – of conformity unto – or transgression of the law of God."

"And, what does that mean, Son?"

"It means that if God tells us to do something and we don't do it, OR if we do something that we aren't supposed to do, then we have sinned."

"That's right. And the Scriptures tell us what we should do when we sin, right?"

Darius shook his head up and down slowly. "We're supposed to say we're sorry?"

"No, we are supposed to confess our sin and admit that it was a transgression of God's law. Then we are to ask God to forgive us. If all you do is say you are sorry, all you are saying is that you feel bad. It doesn't say that you admit you did something that was wrong. When you ask God to forgive you, you are admitting that you have violated His Word and that you are truly going to change your behavior so that it pleases Him. Do you understand?"

"So, when I was snapping Jocelyn with the towel, I was wrong.

"Yes, you were. Tell me, which of God's commands were you violating? Do you know?"

Darius was silent while he thought. "I know that I am to obey Mommy and you, and I know that taking care of the baby meant not hurting her."

"That's why you stopped as soon as your mom walked in. You knew what you were doing was wrong."

Darius shook his head. "I guess I could have really hurt her, and there is the commandment that says not to kill."

His father smiled.

"Dad, are you going to spank me?" Darius asked with quivering lips.

"First of all, you need to pray and ask the Lord to forgive you, because your primary offense was against Him. After that, we can talk about consequences. And, you will need to go and tell your mom and your sister that you know that what you did was wrong and ask them to forgive you. I am going to leave you to have that conversation with God. When I come back in we will talk some more."

His dad got up, kissed his son on the forehead, left the room, and closed the door. Darius closed his eyes and said aloud, "God, please forgive me for my sin of hurting the baby and planning to lie about it. Help me to do the right things."

He got up from his bed, opened his door, and then sat on his bed. His dad came in and sat beside him. "Dad, are you going to spank me?" Darius asked in a whisper.

"No, Son, I'm not. But, your mom and I have talked about it, and we don't want you to continue playing with those action figures that you collect or watch the cartoons they come from. The kind of pretend you do with them isn't godly. We want you to throw them away and not buy any more."

Darius wished that his dad would spank him instead. Give up his action figures? That was more than he could bear. "But, Dad, I asked God to forgive me. Isn't that enough?"

His father continued, "Tomorrow is garbage day and I want you to package those action figures up. We're going to go out tonight and place them in the garbage cans. When you confess your sins, God is faithful and just and forgives them. Isn't that true? Do you remember the rest of the Scripture passage?"

"Yes. It says He cleanses us from unrighteousness."

His father picked Darius up and placed him on his lap. "I know what I'm asking you to do is hard, but your mom and I think this is the correct way to deal with what happened today. We think that those toys aren't good for you. Actually, your mom hasn't liked them for a long time. And, we want you to remember the consequences of your actions. You may not understand or agree with us now, but someday you may think differently. Maybe when you are a dad."

Darius slowly stood up and walked to his dresser. He took out every one of the twelve action figures. These were his favorites; he played with them all the time. Even though the thought of throwing them away hurt so badly, there was a strange sense of relief. He really didn't like how he felt sometimes after he pretended with these toys. It made him feel angry and nasty inside. He just never told anyone before.

Father and son collected the figures and put them in the trash. Then his father told Darius to go see his mother and sister. Darius was relieved to see his mom smile and Jocelyn made that special noise she always made when she saw him. *I guess they still love me*, he thought.

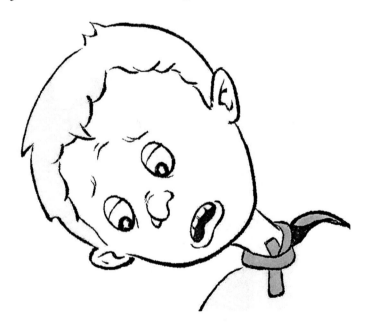

The next morning Darius was up early with his face glued against his bedroom window. He watched the garbage man grab the trashcans and throw the contents into the truck. He had a strange feeling in his stomach – but he knew that his dad had been right. This was the best thing.

Long after the truck drove away, he continued to stare out the window deep in thought about all that had happened. His daydreaming was interrupted when he heard his mother call, "Darius, would you come help me with your sister?"

"Sure, Mom," he called back, grateful that God and his parents were giving him another chance.

Jocelyn's Lesson

Jocelyn was lying in bed angry that she had to take a nap. She hated naps. She hated naps almost as much as she hated having to ride in her booster seat in the car. In fact, Jocelyn hated doing just about anything unless she made the decision by herself.

I only wish I knew how much time an hour and a half is, thought J-Lyn as her brother Darius liked to call her. *That's how much time Mom says I have to nap. I wish it would go by quickly.*

In spite of herself, Jocelyn was soon fast asleep dreaming of running and playing and swimming. When she opened up her eyes, she could tell that time had passed. Her room wasn't as bright as when she first got into bed and she could hear her brother practicing his piano, which meant that it would soon be dinnertime. But she knew better than to just get out of bed and leave her room. Her parents taught her that she always had to ask permission to leave her room after a nap.

"I get up!" she yelled in her loudest voice. No response. "I get up!" she repeated, this time while sitting up. Still nothing. Finally, she stood on her bed and as she jumped up and down shrieked, "I GET UP!!!"

She heard footsteps coming down the hallway; it sounded like a dinosaur. It was Darius. He opened up the door and bellowed, "Mom says you can come out." He was halfway down the hall by the time he finished his sentence.

Jocelyn made her way into the kitchen. Before she could say anything, her mom motioned toward the bathroom and said, "Go use the toilet."

"I don't have to go," she argued, but her mother wouldn't be dissuaded. "Jocelyn, do as you are told."

As she ran to the bathroom she snapped, "I said, 'I don't have to go.'" Once there, she realized that her mother was right – again. Jocelyn didn't like it when her mother was right. In fact, that was one of the things she hated the most.

When she got back to the kitchen, dinner was just about ready. "I didn't have to go, just like I told you," she lied. However, her mother could see that Jocelyn was being spiteful. "What's for dinner?" Jocelyn asked as she pulled the step stool up near where her mother was cooking. "Pasta! Again? I don't want pasta."

Her mother sounded tired when she responded to her brown-haired, brown-eyed daughter. "Nevertheless, we're having pasta." With that, Jocelyn stomped out of the kitchen, grumbling about the menu. She went into the living room where her brother was still practicing and banged on the piano keys.

"Mom, J-Lynn is bothering me. Make her stop!"

Jocelyn just giggled as she stuck out her tongue. "You can't make me."

Darius, looking for any excuse to stop practicing, got up and shoved her. Jocelyn kicked him back and before long, their mother was out of the kitchen with the pasta spoon in hand. "Darius, go back and finish your practice. Jocelyn, stop annoying your brother."

Jocelyn headed to the backyard to play with her Springer Spaniel, Buck. At least her dog understood her. She would often share her innermost thoughts with him, telling him about all the things in life that she hated. He was not one of them. She loved him as much as she loved anyone or anything. Sometimes she felt that Buck was her only friend.

For the next few days, Jocelyn continued to argue anytime she was told to do something, although her mother consistently corrected her bad behavior. Inside, she really didn't like it when she behaved this way, but she also didn't like asking for help. *Mommy always says that I should pray, but I tell God how everyone is mean to me and He doesn't do anything about it.*

On Wednesday afternoon, her mom's bread making day, Jocelyn griped again when it was time for her to take her nap. She and her mom were the only ones in the house. Instead of taking her by the hand and leading her to the bedroom, her mother decided to tell Jocelyn a story. "Jocelyn, come sit down by me. I want to tell you about a little girl."

Jocelyn wasn't sure what to make of all this. She listened carefully and her big brown eyes were fixed on her mom.

Once upon a time there was a little girl...

Jocelyn interrupted, "Is that girl me?"

Her mom continued, *"Once upon a time there was a little girl named Penelope.*

Penelope lived with her mother and father and sisters and brothers.

Jocelyn interrupted again, "Is this a story about me?"

"Now, how could it be about you? You only have one brother and you don't have any sisters. And last I checked your name was Jocelyn. Just listen."

Penelope was a very pretty girl – she had beautiful blonde hair which was very long, almost to her waist.

Because of her outside beauty, when people saw Penelope with her family, they always noticed her first.

But, Penelope wasn't very pretty on the inside. She was one of those people who only cared about herself.

She would yell and scream, cry and pout, and make life miserable for everyone around her if she didn't get her way.

Penelope was only concerned about Penelope.

Jocelyn was strangely silent. Her brown eyes got wider and wider.

So, after people got to know her – even though they considered her very pretty at first, they came to not like her at all.

When Penelope carried on in such a miserable way, her mother and dad would discipline her. At times, she would be spanked for her bad behavior, for the Bible teaches that the rod of discipline is necessary for children. At other times, she would be sent to her room until she could control herself. Then her parents would instruct her from the Bible, and tell her that if she didn't control herself, they would have to discipline and control her.

Jocelyn listened carefully.

However, Penelope would not change her behavior and attitude even after she was punished or sent to her room. She would say she was sorry because her parents insisted on that, but she would not really mean it. She was very good at looking and acting like she meant it. She was very good at saying what she felt people wanted to hear, but when things didn't go her way, she would carry on and act like she had before.

One day, Penelope was sent to her room for deliberately disobeying a well-established rule of the household. To Penelope, that really didn't bother her all that much. After all, in just a little bit she would be allowed to come out. Then she would tell everyone she was sorry, and that would be that.

But this day, no one came to tell her that she could come out. She waited and waited, and no one came. After a long, long time she opened the door just a little to see what her family was doing. She didn't hear a thing. In the past, when it seemed like they would never come, she would open her door and make some noise and someone would come and tell her she could come out. But, they had never taken this long before.

She tiptoed out of her room and walked toward the living room. The house looked very different. No one was there. Her parents had never left her alone before! And, there was not one piece of furniture in the house. The kitchen was empty. The cabinets were empty. There was no refrigerator, no tables, no chairs – no – anything!

She looked around the house. Not one room had furniture in it. The closets were all empty. Now, she was really scared!

Penelope opened the front door. She wanted to know if anyone in the neighborhood knew what had happened to her family. But no one was there. No cars were on the street. Not one house or person could be seen. Not one sound could be heard. Everything looked dull and gray.

She was very scared now and anxiously looked around trying to figure out what to do and where to go.

Suddenly, she saw a thin birch tree with a small blue bird on one of the lower branches. She thought, "I'll ask the bird where everyone is," but realized that it wouldn't do any good to talk to a bird. After all, birds can't understand people.

But this was no ordinary bird. This bird could tell what she was thinking and said, "I can, too, understand people!"

Penelope was astonished but realized that at last she had heard a sound other than her own heart beating and the sound of her footsteps on the ground. "Where did everybody go, Mr. Bird? Where have my mommy and daddy and brothers and sisters gone?"

"They haven't gone anywhere," answered the bird.

"Yes, they have. Yes, they have. They're not anywhere!" she said as tears ran down her cheeks.

The bird looked at Penelope and answered, "Penelope, they haven't gone anywhere. YOU HAVE."

"What do you mean?" cried Penelope. "I'm still here – THEY are gone!"

"I'm afraid you have it wrong, Penelope. YOU are the one who went away. You always lived like you were the only person in the world. When you woke up in the morning, you did not come to the kitchen and greet your mother and ask her how she was. You demanded breakfast or complained about one of your brothers or sisters. When your brother would buy or give you something, you never returned the kindness. You always expected more. You felt that your wants, your needs, your decisions were more important than anyone else's – even God's! You always lived like you were the only person in the world. NOW YOU ARE!

Penelope could not believe what she was hearing. At first, she assumed she must be dreaming, but as before, the bird could tell what she was thinking and said, "No, Penelope, you are definitely not dreaming."

Penelope began to cry and stomp her feet like she used to do any time things didn't go the way she wanted. However, there was no one to hear her, and the bird didn't seem to care. She began to whine and complain about her new situation, but it seemed rather silly since she was the only one listening to herself.

The bird began to move as though he was getting ready to fly. "But you will stay with me, Mr. Bird, won't you?"

"No, Penelope, I was only sent here to tell you where you were. I will be on my way now."

"But, where am I, Mr. Bird? What is the name of this place?" asked Penelope.

"This is called HELL, Penelope. It's a place where people go who are selfish and think only of themselves. Your parents and teachers tried to teach you that kindness, patience, and giving are better than selfishness, impatience, and always taking. But you didn't listen to them."

"But I will listen now. I really will," cried Penelope.

"It's too late. You had your chance, and you did not listen."

Penelope sat down and started to cry. In a very low voice, she called to the bird. "Mr. Bird, can't I, at least, tell my brothers and sisters and friends not to do what I have done? Couldn't I warn them, Mr. Bird?"

"No," replied the bird.

"Couldn't you warn them? Couldn't you tell them not to act like I did?"

"No, Penelope. Why should they listen to you or me when they haven't listened to Moses, the Prophets, or even Jesus Himself?

They have the Bible, Penelope, just as you did. They have teachers and parents just like you did. No, Penelope, if they won't listen to those people, if they won't obey God's Law-Word, they're not going to listen to you. Good-bye, Penelope."

With that, the bird flew away and left Penelope all by herself.

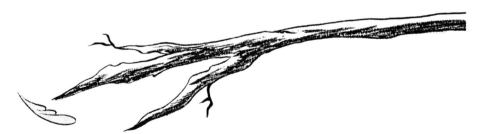

I WONDER WHAT PENELOPE IS DOING TODAY?

Jocelyn looked at her mom as she spoke the last line of the story. Her mother looked at Jocelyn and repeated, "What *do* you think Penelope is doing today?"

Jocelyn started to cry. "I'm sorry, Mommy. I know that I'm a lot like Penelope. But, I don't want to be. Really I don't."

"I know," said her mom as she picked up Jocelyn and placed her on her lap. "The Bible tells us that we do lots of things we know are wrong, but we do them anyway. That's what sin is. And the only way that we can deal with sin…"

Jocelyn interrupted, "Is to get a spanking."

"That's not true, Jocelyn. We do not spank you to wash away your sin. Spankings don't get rid of sins."

"Then why do you and Daddy spank us?"

"So that you can see the consequences of your sin, and hopefully learn not to repeat the same offense again. Only Jesus can take away sins."

"Why didn't the bird give her another chance?"

"Well, the story I told you about Penelope is very much like a parable Jesus told. We refer to it as the parable of the Rich Man and Lazarus. In it, Jesus explains that people are given many, many chances to repent. But, sadly, some just ignore all the teachings of the Bible and choose to go their own way."

Jocelyn jumped from her mother's lap and ran into the bedroom, and returned with the paddle in her hand.

"What's this for?" asked her mother.

"Mommy, there are things I've done and thought about that you and Daddy don't know about. I think I need a lot more spankings. I don't want to go to Hell."

Mrs. Pomeroy smiled on the inside, glad that her daughter had taken her words to heart. "I'm glad you don't want to go to Hell. However, there is much more to obeying God than simply avoiding punishment. When we are obedient to God's rules, we obtain blessings that are not available to those who disobey Him."

Jocelyn's eyes got very wide. "Remember the other day when I was so nasty? I wanted to say I was sorry, but didn't. I should have. And, I lied when I said I did not need to use the bathroom. I'm sorry, Mommy."

"You need to be more than sorry, Jocelyn. You need to ask for forgiveness – to God first and then to me. Being sorry is not enough. You can be sorry you were punished, or you can be sorry you didn't get your way. When you ask for forgiveness, you are admitting you were wrong and acknowledging you need to change direction. It's sort of like what happens when I realize I've gone the wrong way while we are driving and I have to turn around."

Jocelyn smiled, "I guess I need to make a U-turn!"

"That's a great way to put it. You need to make a U-turn. And, you can only do that with God's grace. On your own, you'd just keep acting like you've been acting. I was just like you Jocelyn when I was little. My mother used to say I was going to have a child who was just like me. I wasn't always the easiest person to be around."

"I guess there is hope for me, then, Mommy, because I never ever see you get spanked.

Mrs. Pomeroy picked up the paddle and told Jocelyn to put it back in its place. "I don't think we'll be needing this. Now go to the bathroom and let's get your nap started."

Jocelyn immediately frowned, but thought a second and hugged her mother really hard. "I'm going to go and make my U-turn. You will be here when I wake up, right?"

"Yes, Honey, I will. I love you very much."

When Jocelyn climbed into her bed, she kept thinking about the little girl in the story and how scary Hell was. She wanted to please God; she really did. She was glad God had given her a mommy who cared enough to help her do what was right.

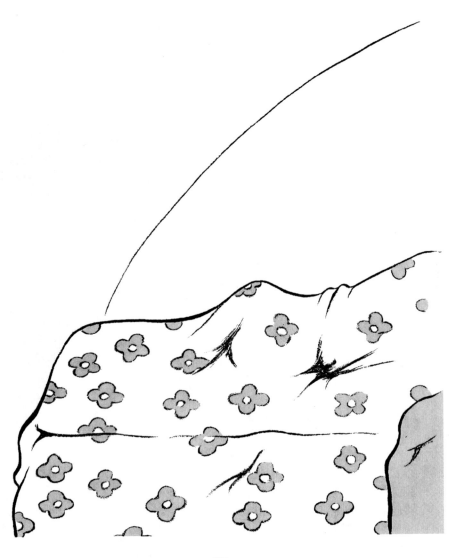

She thought to herself, *Mommy says she was a lot like me when she was little. Just wait until I tell Buck about that! Maybe when I grow up, I'll be a lot like her.*

And with that, she smiled, pulled the covers over her, and fell asleep.

About the author

Andrea Schwartz has written three previous books, *Lessons Learned from Years of Homeschooling*, *The Homeschool Life*, and *The Biblical Trustee Family*. She has been actively involved with homeschooling for over twenty-eight years.

Andrea devotes much of her time and energy writing and lecturing on the Christian philosophy of education and works with both Christian schools and homeschooling parents as a consultant and mentor. She is a regular contributor to the Chalcedon Foundation's bi-monthly magazine, *Faith for All of Life*, and authors the blog www.StartYourHomeschool.com. She co-hosts three podcasts, *His Heartbeat for Women, Notable People,* and Chalcedon's *Law & Liberty.*

Andrea lives in California with her husband of 35 years. She is available for speaking engagements, consultations, or individual mentoring. She can be reached at lessons.learned@yahoo.com.

About the illustrator

Matt Voss is a Savannah College of Art and Design grad and freelance artist living in the San Francisco Bay Area. His website is www.vosshogg.com and he can be reached at vosshogg@aol.com.

CPSIA information can be obtained at www.ICGtesting.com
Printed in the USA
BVOW05s1244020315

389742BV00005B/7/P